God's Tender Words
for Life's Tough Moments

God's
Tender Words
for Life's
Tough Moments

Margaret Houk

Augsburg Books
MINNEAPOLIS

GOD'S TENDER WORDS FOR LIFE'S TOUGH MOMENTS

Large-quantity purchases or custom editions of this book are available at a discount from the publisher. For more information, contact the sales department at Augsburg Fortress, Publishers, 1-800-328-4648, or write to: Sales Director, Augsburg Fortress, Publishers, P.O. Box 1209, Minneapolis, MN 55440-1209.

Cover design by Mira Skocka, cover art by PhotoDisc
Book design by Michelle L. N. Cook

Library of Congress Cataloging-in-Publication Data
Houk, Margaret, 1932-
  God's tender words for life's tough moments / Margaret Houk.
    p. cm.
Includes index.
  ISBN 0-8066-4551-2 (pbk. : alk. paper)
  1. Consolation. I. Title.
BV4905.3 H68 2003
242'.4–dc21   2002013203

The paper used in this publication meets the minimum requirements of American National Standard for Information Sciences–Permanence of Paper for Printed Library Materials, ANSI Z329.48-1984. ⊖ ™

Manufactured in the U.S.A.

07   06   05   04   2   3   4   5   6   7   8   9   10

Dedication

To him for whom I live each day

Contents

Regarding This Book

Life is full of frustrations and stresses. Mistakes and missed communications take their toll. Even the happiest people run into sharp corners and slippery roads in the course of everyday living. Sometimes the bend is slight. (My husband takes offense to something I said.) Sometimes the curve is deep and disabling. (I lost my job today.)

God wants to aid us through these trying times, great or small. We serve our creator best when we keep our emotional ship sailing a steady, confident course. When difficult moments interrupt the journey, nothing can turn our determined, unyielding hearts around as well or as fast as the Lord's own encouraging words in the Bible.

These divine words of strength, love, help, and mercy have moved the hearts of humankind for centuries. May they so comfort and inspire you now as you read this book.

God's Offer
of Gifts
for My Body

Strength When I Am Weak

Sometimes the challenges we human beings face seem overpowering. Will my blood test come out okay? How can I prove my innocence in light of the charges against me? How can I face my friend after the way I hurt her? Will I ever conquer such a deeply rooted bad habit?

We humans are all too aware of our physical and emotional limitations. But God has no limits. God is almighty. Furthermore, God has promised to strengthen us for whatever our life journey brings. In our weaknesses, we can draw the strength we need from God.

"Do not fear, for I am with you; do not be dismayed, for I am your God. I will strengthen you and help you; I will uphold you."
  –Isa. 41:10 NIV
Underneath are the everlasting arms.
  –Deut. 33:27 NIV
The Lord . . . will strengthen and protect you.
  –2 Thess. 3:3 NIV

[He] is able to strengthen you.
  –Rom. 16:25 RSV
Paul said, "I can do all things through Him who strengthens me."
  –Phil. 4:13 NRSV
The joy of the Lord is your strength.
  –Neh. 8:10 NRSV
The Lord said to St. Paul, "My grace is sufficient for you, for [my]
power is made perfect in [your] weakness."
  –2 Cor. 12:9 NRSV

Prayer

Lord, I feel so weak. You are humanity's strength. You can do anything. You have promised to help me in my need. I give myself to you. Let me lean on you. Hold me in your everlasting arms. Protect me from further stress until my energies return.

Undergird me with the joy of knowing and loving you. And remind me constantly that I do not have to be strong–only to live, in whatever state I am, with and for you.

Patience When I Am Impatient

The stresses of modern life often leave us short of patience. I need my computer; why is it taking so long to get the repairs done? Will my toddler ever get past the temper tantrum stage? Why doesn't this elevator move faster? Will my nasty cold ever go away?

When situations try our patience, we need not let them get the best of us. We can handle them better if we approach them with a calm body and a patient mind. God wants that for us, and he will give us instantly the means to face our impatient moments graciously, if we but ask.

Be patient. Establish your hearts. . . . Do not grumble.
    –James 5:8-9 RSV
Love is patient and kind. . . . Love does not demand its own way.
    –1 Cor. 13:4-5 NLT
For everything there is a season, and a time for every matter under heaven.
    –Eccles. 3:1 RSV

Wait for the Lord, and keep to his way, and he will exalt you.
    –Ps. 37:34 NRSV
Be still before the Lord, and wait patiently for him. . . . Those who wait for the Lord shall inherit the land.
    –Ps. 37:7, 9 NRSV
I waited patiently for the Lord; he inclined to me and heard my cry.
    –Ps. 40:1 RSV

Prayer

Lord, in the midst of the hurry and flurry that is my life, slow my steps and settle my mind to come into tune with your timing. Help me to develop the habit of accepting every situation and each moment of life as it comes, knowing you have a purpose for it. Make me grateful rather than impatient, turning my heart around to see the wondrous gifts with which you are constantly gracing my world of family, work, friends, and community.

Calmness When I Am Fretful

Where are my car keys? Oh, no, I forgot to pick up the dry cleaning. My teenager got out of school an hour ago and isn't home yet! Why did I put in such a big lawn that it seems like I must mow it every time I turn around?

Life is full of minor trials and annoyances. Few of us are so easy-going and well-organized that these hurdles don't become unpleasant obstacles from time to time. We can become stewing kettles trying to handle them ourselves, or we can turn them over to God so that we live better the life God wants for us. God understands how we feel, and God will help us do so.

O that I had wings like a dove! I would fly away and be at rest.
    –Ps. 55:6 RSV
Do not fret–it leads only to evil.
    –Ps. 37:8 NRSV
Be still, and know that I am God.
    –Ps. 46:10 RSV

[Some seamen] cried to the Lord in their trouble, and he delivered them; . . . he made the storm be still. . . . Then they were glad because they had quiet.
    –Ps. 107:28-30 RSV

Pause a moment . . . and listen; consider the wonderful things God does.
    –Job 37:14 TEV

My eyes are not raised too high; I do not occupy myself with things too great and too marvelous for me . . . I have calmed and quieted my soul.
    –Ps. 131:1-2 RSV

Prayer

Lord, I cannot serve you well when my body is fretful. Quiet my petulant spirit and fill my mind and heart with the calm stillness of your upholding presence. Grant me the rest that comes from leaning on you, trusting you to take care of the little things that annoy me. Hold me tightly in your compassionate arms, that I may move ahead steadily in a spirit of quiet confidence, humble obedience, gratitude for your blessings, and concern for those around me.

Tranquility When I Am Tense

Will I lose my job in the company's upcoming merger? What will the doctor find on my lab report? Now that the stock market is unstable and my stock values are down, will I have enough money for retirement? Can I make it home safely in this storm?

Experts tell us some tension is good for us, but who needs this much? God knows we frequently have times when peril of some kind looms large. When these occasions come, we need to remember that our destiny is ultimately in God's hands, and God wants us to enjoy life while we are living it.

Have no anxiety about anything, but in everything by prayer and supplication with thanksgiving let your requests be made known to God.

—Phil. 4:6 RSV

[Lord,] you chart the path ahead of me and tell me where to stop and rest.

—Ps. 139:3 NLT

A generation goes, and a generation comes, but the earth remains forever.

—Eccles. 1:4 NRSV

There is a time for everything, and a season for every activity under heaven.

   –Eccles. 3:1 NIV

[God] has made everything beautiful in its time.

   –Eccles. 3:11 NIV

It is fitting to eat and drink and find enjoyment in all the toil with which one toils.

   –Eccles. 5:18 NRSV

Prayer

Lord, I am so tense right now. My body is tight, my mind a concrete block. Help me to relax this rigid self, so that I might find bodily comfort and see you in wise control of all that surrounds me.

   Life is so simple and satisfying when I let go of myself and find you in all things. Lead me, precious Guardian and Protector, through all the perils that threaten my tranquility, so that I might honor, praise, and serve you as I ought.

Rest When I Am Weary

Life today is full of hustle and bustle–jobs, volunteer work, rushing the kids to their piano lessons and confirmation classes, attending church, serving its needs and missions, cleaning the house, servicing the cars, and if we can work it in, taking a nap to make up for an all-too-short night's sleep. Where did the term "leisure time" come from?

Weariness is a familiar syndrome today, created by our activity-heavy lifestyles. Sometimes we can do little about it. But God knows our needs. God wants us to approach life doing our best. Often just a moment of relaxation or even a simple change of pace can refresh our bodies, minds, and spirits. Focusing our hearts on God will quickly get us there.

I lift up my eyes to the hills–from where will my help come? My help comes from the Lord.
  –Ps. 121:1-2 NRSV
Those who live in the shelter of the Most High will find rest in the shadow of the Almighty.
  –Ps. 91:1 NLT
Find rest, O my soul, in God alone.
  –Ps. 62:5 NIV

Jesus said, "Come to me, all you that are weary and are carrying heavy burdens, and I will give you rest."
    –Matt. 11:28 NRSV
Cast your burden on the Lord, and he will sustain you.
    –Ps. 55:22 RSV
Cast all your anxieties on him, for he cares about you.
    –1 Pet. 5:7 RSV

Prayer

I am so tired, Lord. Life is such a burden at times. But it need not be. No moment spent with you is ever weighed down by boredom, fatigue, or anxiety. Your glorious presence always exhilarates me. Your merciful love lifts my weary heart. Your promise to take on all my anxieties overwhelms with joyful relief my weary soul.

Let your Holy Spirit indwell me, Lord, that I may be encouraged and sustained. I can rest assured that your everlasting arms will carry me wherever I need to go. With humble thanks, I raise to you my head, my hands, and my heart in praise and gratitude for your steadfast faithfulness toward me.

Focus When I Am Out-of-Sorts

Do you feel pulled in different directions, trying to find a path through the thick forest? Are the problems and trials of life leaving you in a daze? Did you have trouble getting "with it" today, after a poor night's sleep? Or perhaps problems with your children have you gritting your teeth.

We all have days and times like this. It's not fun, being out-of-sorts with those we love and our familiar routines. God loves us and understands our need to refocus. If we put our distress in God's hands, God will quickly pull our life's walk back on track, and all other matters will fall into place.

This is the assurance we have in approaching God: that if we ask anything according to his will, he hears us. And . . . we know that we have what we asked of him.
    –1 John 5:14-15 NIV
Trust in the Lord with all your heart, and do not rely on your own insight.
    –Prov. 3:5 RSV
The Lord takes thought for me.
    –Ps. 40:17 NRSV

[The Lord] leads me in right paths for his name's sake.
    –Ps. 23:3 NRSV
What does the Lord require of you but to do justice, and to love
kindness, and to walk humbly with your God?
    –Mic. 6:8 RSV
Seek the welfare of the [place] where I have sent you, . . . and pray to
the Lord on its behalf, for in its welfare you will find your welfare.
    –Jer. 29:7 RSV

Prayer

Some days it seems like it just doesn't pay to get up, Lord. I can't find solid ground to stand on . . . that is, until I turn to you, my creator God, my loving savior, my very reason for being and living.

Help me to find you in the fog, Lord. Send your Holy Spirit to point the way ahead for me. And always abide in my heart, so that my life this day might witness to your will and radiate your unconditional love to whomever I meet.

Composure When I Am Angry

How can my boss make such a ridiculous request of me? My spouse is being so impossible! Why did the car have to break down right now, when I can't afford repair bills? The children haven't done their chores again!

Whatever the source of our hotheadedness, anger is not good for our bodies, minds, or souls. It raises our blood pressure, pushes our mental states beyond usual control, and stresses our relationships with God and others, sometimes to the point of endangerment. We need not let this happen. God in his Holy Scriptures provides many messages to help us regain and maintain our composure.

Do not let the sun go down while you are still angry, and do not give the devil a foothold.
    –Eph. 4:26-27 NIV
A soft answer turns away wrath, but a harsh word stirs up anger.
    –Prov. 15:1 RSV
As churning the milk produces butter, . . . so stirring up anger produces strife.
    –Prov. 30:33 NIV

Be quick to listen, slow to speak, and slow to get angry. Your anger can never make things right in God's sight.
    –James 1:19-20 NLT
Forsake wrath. . . . [for] the meek shall inherit the land, and delight themselves in abundant prosperity.
    –Ps. 37:8, 11 NRSV
Create in me a clean heart, O God, and put a new and right spirit within me.
    –Ps. 51:10 NRSV

Prayer

It's so easy for us to get angry, Lord. Accusations fly, tempers flare, bitterness reigns, and the poisonous climate stifles the air. And we–the people I care about and those who care about me–turn away from each other in cold, miserable isolation.

When anger arises, Lord, help me to stop in my tracks, pause and think about what I am doing, pray for your insight, and have you turn my heart from angry bitterness to understanding love. Even as you have loved me even at my worst moments, so I too with your help can love any other human being, regardless of the cause of the hurt I experienced or who is at fault.

Restoration When I Am Overwhelmed

My job is just too demanding! The workload of my job, family, household responsibilities, and lugging the kids to choir practice and karate sessions are taking too heavy a toll. Added to everything else I have to do, helping my mother with her disabling illness is draining all the energy from my veins and heart.

It would be nice if life came in orderly boxes, all the same size, but it doesn't. Sometimes we get lifts, other times setbacks. Some boxes are big, some little. Some overwhelm us. But God stands with us through them all. God is there when our babies are born and when the roof caves in. Whatever our overwhelming situation, God can and will restore us.

Hear my prayer, O Lord; let my cry come to you. Do not hide your face from me in the day of my distress. Incline your ear to me; answer me speedily.
—Ps. 102:1-2 NRSV

Lead me to the rock that is higher than I.
—Ps. 61:2 NRSV

My spirit faints within me; my heart within me is appalled. . . . I stretch out my hands to you; my soul thirsts for you like a parched land. Answer me quickly, O Lord.
—Ps. 143:4, 6-7 NRSV

The Lord has heard my supplication; the Lord accepts my prayer.
    –Ps. 6:9 NRSV
With God all things are possible.
    –Matt. 19:26 NIV
The Lord is my shepherd. . . . He leads me beside still waters; he restores my soul.
    –Ps. 23:1-3 NRSV

Prayer

The ground is sinking under my feet, Lord. You have said you will never give me more than I can handle, but it certainly feels right now as though that you are overestimating my resources.

How can I go on? By letting you take my overwhelming load onto your shoulders. Help me climb onto you, my rock. Quench my thirst with your spiritual life-giving water. Replenish me with strength of heart. And lead me swiftly out of this bleak wilderness, restoring me to a comfortable life once again alongside still waters.

God's Offer
of Gifts
for My Mind

Peace of Mind When I Am Troubled

Troubles are unwanted dips in the cycles of life. My car broke down yesterday. I had an argument with my teenage son. My company notified us that it is going to lay off some employees. I woke up this morning with a pain in my stomach.

Troubles come and go. They may be inevitable. They may be hard to live with while they're here. But we need not allow them to unsettle us for long. God wants us to have peace of mind and heart continuously. In fact, God promises it to us.

Do not let your hearts be troubled.
    –John 14:1 NRSV
God is . . . a very present help in trouble.
    –Ps. 46:1 NRSV
The Lord is good, a refuge in times of trouble. He cares for those who trust in him.
    –Nah. 1:7 NIV
The Lord [will] turn his face toward you and give you peace.
    –Num. 6:26 NIV

Jesus said, "My peace I give to you . . . not [temporary peace,] as the world gives."
    –John 14:27 NRSV
The peace of God . . . passes all understanding.
    –Phil. 4:7 RSV
Those of steadfast mind you [God] keep in peace . . . because they trust in you.
    –Isa. 26:3 NRSV

Prayer

Lord, it is so easy to get carried away by little things in life–distractions, irritations, and worries. I know you are there for me and that you promised to meet all of my needs. You have promised me *perfect* peace if I turn everything over to you, confident that you are working your will in every situation–good or bad–that interrupts the normal routine of my life.

I need peace. I want your kind of peace. Lord, help me to stay open to the serenity that is always there, waiting for me, in your loving arms. Amen

Certainty When I Am Unsure

Is this new job right for me? Would I be happy in a condo? I like this person I've been dating, but could we make a marriage work? How much money will it take for me to retire comfortably?

If life came with a complete manual of instructions, we might be able to make choices confidently. It doesn't, of course. We don't even understand ourselves perfectly, much less others. But God can guide us when we are in doubt. In fact, God leading is the only road that guarantees us we are on the right track.

The wisdom from above is first pure, then peaceable, gentle, open to reason, full of mercy and good fruits, without uncertainty or insincerity.
   –James 3:17 RSV
If any of you is lacking in wisdom, ask God. . . . But ask in faith, never doubting, for the one who doubts is like a wave of the sea, driven and tossed by the wind.
   –James 1:5-6 NRSV
O Lord, . . . you hear my voice; . . . I plead my case to you, and watch.
   –Ps. 5:3 NRSV

Though we stumble, we shall not fall headlong, for the Lord holds us by the hand.

   –Ps. 37:24 NRSV

My heart is steadfast, O God, my heart is steadfast.

   –Ps. 57:7 NRSV

Keep my steps steady according to your promise, and never let iniquity have dominion over me.

   –Ps. 119:133 NRSV

Prayer

I am not sure what to do, Lord. Am I making the right choices? Will things work out satisfactorily for me?

   Of course they will, if I lean on you. They always do, even when the choice looks wrong at the time. Dissolve my doubts, Lord. Lead me with your strong, steady hand so that I do not stumble and fall or head off in a wrong direction. Give me the assurance that I am on your road, not mine. And may your never-failing wisdom bring me the fruits of peace and joy.

Perseverance When I Am Tempted to Quit

I am bored to death with this project! Must I go on? I never asked for this task, so why should I finish it? When I volunteered, I didn't realize how much time it would take. This responsibility is more than I bargained for; why did I ever get into it?

When the waters of responsibility rise dauntingly high, we may be tempted to think we are in over our heads. At times we are. But sometimes we must admit we are just plain lazy. Other times God gives us a job that is tedious or looks too big for us. When these things happen God will help us persevere, if we ask. If and when we do so, God promises to bless us for our faithfulness.

Jesus said, "Ask and it will be given to you; seek and you will find; knock and the door will be opened to you."
    –Matt. 7:7 NIV
Be careful then how you live, . . . making the most of the time.
    –Eph. 5:15-16 NRSV
Being lazy will make you poor, but hard work will make you rich.
    –Prov. 10:4 TEV

Let us hold true to what we have attained.
    –Phil. 3:16 RSV
Perseverance must finish its work so that you may be mature and complete.
    –James 1:4 NIV
You need to persevere so . . . you will receive what [God] has promised.
    –Heb. 10:36 NIV

Prayer

Help me, Lord, to complete what I have begun. You do not want me to be a quitter, and I don't either. But this responsibility is so hard to face right now.

You have promised you will help me to finish. You have promised I will be blessed for doing so. I want your help. I crave your blessings in my life. Please give me the heart to go on and, when the rewards for persevering come, a humble spirit of grateful thanks and joyful appreciation.

Determination When I Am Indecisive

I don't know whether to move or to stay where I am. Should I take on this important volunteer job right now? Is college the right direction for my child? Is this the right time to trade in my car for a newer, more reliable model?

Life is full of decisions. Contrary to popular opinion, decision making is not always fun or easy. Things could turn out better or worse. But when we include the Lord in all of our decision making, asking that *God's* will be done, we need never have regrets.

Let God transform you into a new person by changing the way you think. Then you will know what God wants you to do.
    –Rom. 12:2 NLT
Our steps are made firm by the Lord, when he delights in our way.
    –Ps. 37:23 NRSV
This we will do if God permits.
    –Heb. 6:3 RSV

Take a new grip with your tired hands and stand firm on your shaky legs. Mark out a straight path for your feet. Then those who follow you . . . will not stumble and fall but will become strong.
    –Heb. 12:12-13 NLT
In everything do to others as you would have them do to you.
    –Matt. 7:12 NRSV

Prayer

Everywhere I turn, decisions need to be made. How can I always know which is the best choice? By turning all of them over to you, Lord.

Give me a mindset to look automatically to you for answers, my dear Lord and master. Then my steps will be sure, my hands will be steady, and my chosen paths will work for the good of those around me as well as myself. Then I will become a strong, effective witness to what your love and guidance can accomplish in the lives of believers.

Direction When I Am Confused

Life in today's world is complex. Sometimes we don't know which way to turn. Some of us wonder what we are doing in such a dull job with no future. Those of us who are housebound often find our days stretch on endlessly, leading us to ask, "What's the point?" We who are caught up in a constant whirlwind of activity seek a clearing in the clouds of perpetual busyness.

God has a road map for each person's life and for every situation in our lives. We find direction by prayerfully seeking God's will for us and then looking around for it right where we are, right now.

Unless the Lord builds the house, those who build it labor in vain.
    –Ps. 127:1 RSV
Commit your way to the Lord; trust in him, and he will act.
    –Ps. 37:5 RSV
Whether you turn to the right or to the left, your ears will hear a voice behind you, saying, "This is the way; walk in it."
    –Isa. 30:21 NIV

Lead a life worthy of God.
  −1 Thess. 2:12 RSV
O send out your light and your truth; let them lead me.
  −Ps. 43:3 NRSV
Your word is a lamp to my feet and a light to my path.
  −Ps. 119:105 NRSV

Prayer

Lord, I need to find my way through the dense woods of my life. I know you have a path for me, but I can't see it right now. Give me patience, Lord, to wait until the answers come, the fortitude to hold strong in the meantime, and the vision to look past my human blinders and see those answers that are already all around me.

Be with me, Lord, and guide me. Reassure me constantly of your love, your presence, and the promise of your direction while I walk this earthly road.

Wisdom When I Lack Understanding

Why did my teenager experiment with drugs, after all the warnings and education we gave? I should have gotten that promotion at work; I am better qualified. My sister shouldn't have had a heart attack; she did everything right: exercise, healthy diet, good health care.

Even when we think we have everything under control, life throws boomerangs at us. There is no explanation for why some things happen. But God is there, knowing us well and discerning what each of us needs. God has a plan in mind for all that occurs, and God promises to share the knowledge and wisdom behind it for the asking.

If any of you is lacking wisdom, ask God, who gives to all generously and ungrudgingly, and it will be given you. But ask in faith, never doubting.
    –James 1:5-6 NRSV
The fear of the Lord is the beginning of knowledge.
    –Prov. 1:7 NRSV

[Lord], in your light we see light.
    –Ps. 36:9 NRSV

My child, if you accept my words and treasure up my command-ments, . . . if you indeed cry out for insight, and raise your voice for understanding; . . . then you will . . . find the knowledge of God.

Then you will understand righteousness and justice and equity, every good path; for wisdom will come into your heart, and knowledge will be pleasant to your soul; prudence will watch over you; and understanding will guard you.
    –Prov. 2:1, 3, 5, 9-11 NRSV

Prayer

Lord, I don't understand why some things happen the way they do. Sometimes they don't make sense. But you know what is going on and why. I know that, for believers, all things work together for good in your world. Enlighten me. Grace me with your knowledge and insight, if it be your will. But mostly, just walk with me through the dark alleys and along the foggy paths until understanding comes, that I may be your faithful servant always.

Courage When I Am Afraid

Will I lose my job in the upcoming layoff? Will our country undergo another major terrorist attack? Will a few disturbed students shoot out their frustrations at my child's school? Is that stalker in our city going to rape and kill someone I know or even me?

Sometimes years pass us by in relative comfort. Then something happens that shakes us to our very soul. But we live in a world poisoned by evil, and our need to live in God's trust has never been situational. God can and will give us the courage to face whatever occurs. God is our constant strength, our ever-present song.

The Lord is my light and my salvation; whom shall I fear?
    –Ps. 27:1 NRSV
God will put his angels in charge of you to protect you wherever you go.
    –Ps. 91:11 TEV
The Lord said, "Do not fear, for I am with you, do not be afraid, for I am your God."
    –Is. 41:10 NRSV

[Lord], you are a hiding place for me; you preserve me from trouble.
    –Ps. 32:7 NRSV
When my spirit is [afraid], you know my way, [Lord]. . . . You are my refuge.
    –Ps. 142:3, 5 NRSV
Even though I walk through the darkest valley, I fear no evil; for you are with me.
    –Ps. 23:4 NRSV

Prayer

Lord, the world is a fearful place. Evil is all around us, often hiding under an ordinary-looking coat. But it cannot hide from you. You know my fear. Replace it with godly trust and courage, so that I may do your work in this world fearlessly, honorably, and lovingly.

Sufficiency When I Am Financially Stressed

My credit cards are maxed out, and I still can't meet my bills. Why did this dental emergency have to come along right now? Mother is in a hospital one thousand miles away, and I can't afford to fly out to be with her. Insurance is not going to cover all the damage caused by this storm.

Unplanned expenses, unexpected emergencies, or just plain poor management can devastate our finances. We may even ask, "God, I tried so hard to handle my money well. Why did you let this happen?" We can't know God's mind. But we do know God promises to take care of us and that God has an uncanny way of meeting urgent needs in unexpected ways. Our job is to pray for God's providence, trusting God's faithfulness.

God will meet all your needs.
    –Phil 4:19 NIV
Bring the full tithes into the storehouse . . . and thereby put me to the test, says the Lord of hosts, if I will not open the windows of heaven for you and pour down for you an overflowing blessing.
    –Mal. 3:10 RSV

God is able to provide you with every blessing in abundance, so that you may always have enough of everything.
    –2 Cor. 9:8 RSV
Give us this day our daily bread.
    –Matt. 6:11 NRSV
Feed me with the food that is my portion.
    –Prov. 30:8 NASB
Give thanks in all circumstances, for this is God's will for you in Christ Jesus.
    –1 Thess. 5:18 NIV

Prayer

In a moneyed economy it is hard to exist when one is low on cash. But you know that, Lord. Help me and my family through this present urgent need. Reassure me steadily that you are watching over us and will see that we get what we truly need. Help me to handle money and the other earthly goods you provide carefully and wisely. And grant me the grace to live patiently and cheerfully within the means that your gifts allow. Mostly, give me a heart grateful for all of the many blessings you already lovingly provide.

Self-Assurance When I Feel Inadequate

My family expects me to do everything; don't they realize how impossible that is? How will I ever learn this complicated computer program? I'm not mechanical; I can't handle these repair tools. I'm not sure my health will enable me to keep working until I retire.

Does the road ahead look too hard for you? Is the mountain range too vast? If you trust, God will carry you over the mountain passes, across the raging rivers, through any storms, and around the boulders. God is the giver of all gifts, and God knows the challenges our weaknesses present. Our best road is God's road. Resting in God, we can be all God wants us to be. And we need be nothing more.

The Lord God is a sun and shield. . . . No good thing does the Lord withhold from those who walk uprightly.
    –Ps. 84:11 NRSV
Commit your way to the Lord; trust in him and he will . . . make your righteousness shine like the dawn, the justice of your cause like the noonday sun.
    –Ps. 37:5-6 NIV

[The Lord] gives power to the faint, and strengthens the powerless.
    –Is. 40:29 NRSV
Strengthen me according to your word.
    –Ps. 119:28 NRSV
I can do all things through him who strengthens me.
    –Phil. 4:13 NRSV
*My health may fail, and my spirit may grow weak, but God remains
the strength of my heart; he is mine forever.*
    –Ps. 73:26 NLT

Prayer

What do I do and where do I go, Lord, when the skyscraper of my
life blocks your radiant sunshine? I must turn my mind to seeing
what you see, my ears to hearing your wise words, my heart to
trusting in you, and my lips to singing your praises. Show me your
road for me, Lord, and reassure me steadily that your strength will
uphold me and your loving arms will guide and accompany me as
I walk along the way. For then I can walk with confidence and self-
assurance.

God's Offer
of Gifts
for My Spirit

Serenity When I Am Worried

Will my lab tests come out okay? Can my daughter's troubled marriage be saved? Will the hurricane barreling this way destroy our house? Can I live on my unemployment check until I get another job?

In a complex society like ours, much can go wrong. We depend heavily on a knowledgeable health care system, sophisticated weather forecasters, a vast insurance network, and an elaborate government social program to undergird our lives. But nothing is truly certain in life. Only God can meet our every need. God wants to. We need not worry. If God promises us, we can trust.

Don't worry about everyday life–whether you have enough food to eat or clothes to wear. . . . Look at the ravens. They don't need to plant or harvest or put food in barns because God feeds them. And you are far more valuable to him than any birds!
  –Luke 12:22, 24 NLT
Do not worry about tomorrow, for tomorrow will bring worries of its own. Today's trouble is enough for today.
  –Matt. 6:34 NRSV

Have no anxiety about anything, but in everything by prayer and supplication with thanksgiving let your requests be made known to God. And the peace of God, which passes all understanding, will keep your hearts and your minds in Christ Jesus.

   –Phil. 4:6-7 RSV

Bless the Lord, my soul, and do not forget all his benefits. . . . [He] satisfies you with good as long as you live.

   –Ps. 103:2, 5 NRSV

Prayer

Something has gone wrong in my life, Lord, and I just can't help but worry. Or is that true? You have said you will always to be there for me. I can choose instead to trust that promise. I can depend on you to provide what I need. I can lean on you for the resources I need to meet any problem. Instead of wasting my energy on fruitless anxieties, I can turn my mind and heart around, loving and praising and rejoicing in you, my everlasting provider and friend. Please help me to do so.

Love When I Feel Unloved

My husband forgot my birthday. My friends didn't invite me to their party. My teenager screamed at me, ran out, and slammed the door. I wonder if I'll ever get past the pain of this divorce.

We depend on our relatives and friends to love us in all situations and to care about our needs, but they don't always. Sometimes they are thoughtless, neglectful, or even downright hateful. But sometimes we are, too. God is the only being who loves us in all circumstances, despite ourselves. We can always find our great need for unconditional love in God–our steadfast, faithful Lord–any time, any place.

How precious is your steadfast love, O God!
    –Ps. 36:7 NRSV
Let me hear of your steadfast love in the morning.
    –Ps. 143:8 NRSV
For as the heavens are high above the earth, so great is [God's] steadfast love toward those who fear him.
    –Ps. 103:11 NRSV
Christ Jesus has made me his own.
    –Phil. 3:12 NRSV

Jesus says, "As the Father has loved me, so I have loved you; abide in my love."
  –John 15:9 NRSV
"Greater love has no one than this, that one lay down his life for his friends."
  –John 15:13 NIV
"[It is] the will of him who sent me, . . . that I should not lose any of all those he has given me."
  –John 6:38-39 TEV

Prayer

At the moment I don't know if *anyone* around me is concerned about me or how I feel. But you care, Lord. Magnanimous Father that you are, you always listen carefully and love me perfectly. How can I ever thank you enough for being the wonderful God that you are and for loving me so deeply? Love generates love in return. Please turn my ailing heart around so I can focus on loving your people dearly and unconditionally, just as you have loved me.

Joy When I Am Sad

A friend of mine was diagnosed with cancer. I lost all my family records in our flooded basement. My son didn't score well on his achievement test at school. My favorite pastor left our church for placement elsewhere.

Sad moments come into everyone's life. We can't stop them. We can't even control most of them. But we can learn to look for God in the midst of our sadness. God has a reason for all that happens. And God has promised to help us root our everyday lives in something more solid–everlasting joy, the abundant happiness that comes with knowing, loving, and trusting God completely, at all times and in all things.

The ransomed of the Lord . . . shall obtain joy and gladness, and sorrow and sighing shall flee away.
  –Isa. 51:11 NRSV
The steadfast love of the Lord never ceases, his mercies never come to an end; they are new every morning.
  –Lam. 3:22-23 NRSV
Jesus said, "I am the gate. Whoever enters by me will be saved. . . . I came that [my followers] may have life, and have it abundantly."
  –John 10:9-10 NRSV

"I have said these things to you so that my joy may be in you, and that your joy may be complete."
   –John 15:11 NRSV
"You have pain now; but I will see you again, and your hearts will rejoice, and no one will take your joy from you."
   –John 16:22, 24 NRSV
You [Lord] will make me full of gladness with your presence.
   –Acts 2:28 NRSV

Prayer

A painful sadness has come into my life, Lord, and my heart is so heavy right now. But you never promised us every day would be a sunny day on this side of heaven. Though sadness is my lot for the moment, lift my heart with your loving hands and turn it to gladness. May I come to rejoice again soon in the joy that is found solely in loving and trusting you completely.

Encouragement When I Am Discouraged

Things haven't been working out for me lately. I can't seem to learn how to use my electronic organizer. My family is scattering, and we don't have time for each other anymore. My job is going nowhere. When we moved recently, I hoped to make new friends quickly, but it just isn't happening.

The rhythm of life is not steady or smooth. Things go well for awhile, then they seem to fall apart for a time. But God is with us in our difficult times as well as our good ones. God's world is much bigger than ours. God can and will lift us lovingly over every valley, with grace, just for the asking.

Hold fast . . . , and wait continually for your God.
    –Hos. 12:6 RSV
In his heart a man plans his course, but the Lord determines his steps.
    –Prov. 16:9 NIV
In everything God works for good with those who love him.
    –Rom. 8:28 RSV

Trust in the Lord with all your heart and lean not on your own understanding; in all your ways acknowledge him, and he will make your paths straight.

    –Prov. 3:5 NIV

[Lord,] let your good spirit lead me on a level path.

    –Ps. 143:10 NRSV

Surely goodness and mercy shall follow me all the days of my life, and I shall dwell in the house of the Lord my whole life long.

    –Ps. 23:6 NRSV

Prayer

I sure can't see where my life is going right now, Lord. Things are not good, and I don't know how to fix them. But you do. You want me to hold fast to you and trust you to clear the murky skies so I can see your route for me. Be with me, Lord. Lift me. Encourage me. And walk me toward the path you have in mind for me as I reach out in dependence, gratitude for your blessings, and love.

A Lift When I Feel Dejected

I'm in a deep rut, and I can't seem to pull myself out. Ever since I fought with my best friend, life has been one dark day after another. Why do I have to keep going in this endless job? I wake up every day with a headache, and I'm beginning to think it will never go away.

Depression is very common today. Lasting, severe depression needs clinical treatment. But when we are feeling a little sad, it sometimes helps to turn our minds and spirits over to God's handling for prompt healing. The Lord wants emotional health for us. We serve God better when our spirits are alive and well, and God welcomes our regrets for uplift when we feel dejected.

To you, O Lord, I lift up my soul.... You are the God of my salvation.
　　–Ps. 25:1, 5 NRSV
You, O Lord, are my hope.
　　–Ps. 71:5 NRSV
Let the light of your face shine on [me], O Lord!
　　–Ps. 4:6 NRSV

Gladden the soul of your servant.
    –Ps. 86:4 NRSV
David said, "I will exalt you, O Lord, for you lifted me out of the depths. . . . I called to you for help and you healed me."
    –Ps. 30:1-2 NIV
Jesus said, "I came that [you] may have life, and have it abundantly."
    –John 10:10 NRSV

Prayer

It's no fun living in a deep pit, Lord, and it's very hard to pull myself out. I look to you for help and healing. Your strength is made perfect in my weakness.

Lift my spirits, Lord, that I may dwell in your sunshine once more and taste the life of abundant joy Jesus wants for me. Then I will be able to praise you as I ought, serve you with greater energy, and proclaim your gracious love to the rooftops.

Confidence When I Feel Vulnerable

I reported a discrimination problem at work and could lose my job because of it. I told someone a secret, and it might backfire on me. I drove when my doctor said I shouldn't; I caused an accident and now must go to trial.

Compromising situations can get us into many kinds of trouble, some deserved, some not. Regardless of our intent, God can and will be with us through these difficult times. God knows our needs and meets them. God will give us the means to face them courageously. We can always count on God to be our support system, to remain our refuge and strength, to become our confidence.

The Lord watches over you–the Lord is your shade at your right hand; the sun will not harm you by day, nor the moon by night. . . . The Lord will watch over your coming and going both now and forevermore.
    –Ps. 121:5-6, 8 NIV
O Lord, you have searched me and known me. You know when I sit down and when I rise up; you discern my thoughts from far away. You search out my path and my lying down, and are acquainted with all my ways.
    –Ps. 139:1-3 NRSV

In the shadow of your wings I will take refuge, until the destroying storms pass by.
  –Ps. 57:1 NRSV
Save me, O Lord, from my enemies.
  –Ps. 143:9 NRSV
Deliver [me] from evil.
  –Matt. 6:13 RSV
I will lie down and sleep in peace, for you alone, O Lord, make me dwell in safety.
  –Ps. 4:8 NIV

Prayer

Regardless of the nature of the vulture that presently threatens my peace of mind, Lord, I know that you are steadfast in your love for me. You know if I've done right or wrong, and where I've erred, and you have forgiven me. May your comforting presence in my life give me the confidence to lift up my head and carry on, making amends where I've done wrong and knowing I am honoring you if I was doing what is right in your eyes. My precious Lord, thank you for being my confidence.

Consolation When I Am Anguished

How will I ever live with this personal injury accident I caused? I so regret leaving for military duty; I wasn't there when my son was hurt and hospitalized. I never realized that the effects of my divorce would linger so long on members of my family. I wish I would have done more over the years to help addicted people and those living in abject poverty.

Anguish is all around us. Sometimes we cause it. Sometimes others do. Sometimes circumstances cause this kind of grief. But it all hurts, just the same. When anguished moments come, God is always there to console us with God's presence, bringing along God's unfailing love, help, and healing.

My flesh and my heart may fail, but God is the strength of my heart and my portion for ever.
    –Ps. 73:26 RSV
Trouble and distress have come upon me, but your commands are my delight.
    –Ps. 119:143 NIV
Comfort, O comfort my people, says your God.
    –Isa. 40:1 NRSV

When you go through deep waters and great trouble, I will be with you. When you go through rivers of difficulty, you will not drown!
    –Isa. 43:2 NLT
"Though the mountains be shaken and the hills be removed, yet my unfailing love for you will not be shaken nor my covenant of peace be removed," says the Lord.
    –Isa. 54:10 NIV
The Lord bless you and keep you; the Lord make his face to shine upon you, and be gracious to you; the Lord lift up his countenance upon you, and give you peace.
    –Num. 6:24-26 NRSV

Prayer

The world is not a pretty place. People get sick or hurt. People hurt each other. I, too, cause others grief from time to time. But this same world is yours, Lord. You created it.

We may not always understand why hurt and pain occur, but we are assured that you are always there, responding to our anguish with divine consolation, mercy, and love. Whether I am innocent or guilty, please bring me your compassionate love and healing and give me the vision to see where I in turn can console and comfort others.

Help When I Feel Helpless

My health condition has deteriorated, and there is nothing more doctors can do about it. My child has broken the law and now must go to jail. My mother has been widowed, and I live too far away to be much help to her. We are moving, and I will soon lose many dear friends.

Some life situations leave us feeling helpless. The lesser of two evils is still an evil. God knows we are hurting and cares. God hurts with us. God wants us to request help. Somehow, walking the rough and painful road with God makes our walk a little easier.

The Lord . . . is our help and shield.
   –Ps. 33:20 NRSV
O Lord, do not be far away! O my help, come quickly to my aid!
   –Ps. 22:19 NRSV
Blessed is the man whose strength is in You.
   –Ps. 84:5 NASB
There appeared to [Jesus] an angel from heaven, strengthening him.
   –Luke 22:43 RSV

When you pass through the waters, I will be with you; and when you pass through the rivers, they will not sweep over you. When you walk through the fire, you will not be burned ... for I am the Lord, your God, ... your Savior.
   –Isa. 43:2-3 NIV

I am convinced that neither death nor life, neither angels nor demons, neither the present nor the future, nor any powers, neither height nor depth, nor anything else in all creation, will be able to separate us from the love of God that is in Christ Jesus our Lord.
   –Rom. 8:38 NIV

Prayer

What can I do? Nothing. Where can I find a way out? I can't. I see no way through the troubled waters around me, Lord. Hear my plea for help. You alone are always there, meeting my every need, regardless of the difficulty I am dealing with. Your loving embrace will carry me through. I need you now. I trust you, Lord. I love you, Lord. Please accept and nurture my surrendered heart.

Contentment When I Am Jealous or Envious

My brother just bought a lovely new home; I wish we could afford something like that. There's a tall, striking woman at church who wears gorgeous clothes; I wish I looked more like her. Why do some families bear several children so easily, when we have so much trouble trying to conceive just one?

It's said so often: "Life isn't fair." And it isn't. Life is especially hard when the things we want most are the hardest to come by. But we need not worry. The Lord knows our wants. More importantly, God knows our inner needs. If we trust in God's judgment, God's plan for us will bring us contentment, leading to greater joy than following our own ways would.

Do not fret over those who prosper in their way.
    –Ps. 37:7 NRSV
Those who love money will never have enough. . . . The more you have, the more people come to help you spend it.
    –Eccles. 5:10-11 NLT
Do not store up for yourselves treasures on earth, where moth and rust consume and where thieves break in and steal; but store up for yourselves treasures in heaven. . . . For where your treasure is, there your heart will be.
    –Matt. 6:19-21 NRSV

A heart at peace gives life to the body, but envy rots the bones.
  –Prov. 14:30 NIV
The world passes away, and the lust of it; but [the person] who does the will of God abides forever.
  –1 John 2:17 RSV
Godliness with contentment is great gain.
  –1 Tim. 6:6 NIV

Prayer

We humans so enjoy the blessings you give, Lord, but we never seem to have enough. Or that's what we like to think. In truth, I have far more than I need and often lack gratitude for what you do give. And I do not always recognize what I truly need for genuine happiness. Give me what you want for me, Lord, and a grateful heart along with it, that I may keep my priorities straight, thanking and praising you for all that I am and have.

God's Offer
of Gifts
for My Soul

Support When I Am Tempted

My male friend is married, but my husband doesn't understand me and this friend is much easier to talk to. I'd like to take all the expenses for my trip off my income tax; everybody does it. I can't afford to upgrade my software, but all my friends have the new version, maybe I could just "borrow" it from one of them.

In our advertising-saturated world, resisting temptation requires constant self-control. So does living in a society that says commitment to relationships is not as important as being happy. How do we counteract these seductive forces? By keeping our priorities focused on the Lord's. God's Commandments show us what will make us most happy and blessed, and God has promised to help us keep them.

The devil prowls around, looking for someone to devour. Resist him.
    −1 Pet. 5:8-9 NRSV
Keep alert and pray. Otherwise temptation will overpower you. For though the spirit is willing enough, the body is weak!
    −Matt. 26:41 NLT

God is faithful. He will keep the temptation from becoming so strong that you can't stand up against it. When you are tempted, he will show you a way out so that you will not give in to it.

　　–1 Cor. 10:13 NLT

Observe [God's laws] carefully, for this will show your wisdom and understanding to the nations [around you].

　　–Deut. 4:6 NIV

Those who have clean hands and pure hearts ... will receive blessing from the Lord.

　　–Ps. 24:4-5 NRSV

Prayer

Lord, the values in this world look so appealing at times. The media rarely show us the problems they bring. I know in my heart that your ways are best, but I am human. Sometimes following your Commandments is hard. Lead me not into temptation. Keep my eyes focused on your laws and my heart dedicated to serving you faithfully, that I may honor you in all that I do.

Communion with God When I Feel Spiritually Out of Touch

God doesn't seem near anymore. I can't feel his presence, and sometimes I have difficulty believing he truly cares about me. I am a believer; why isn't he automatically here with me? I walk around, and all I see are nothing but the trappings of life. I look up, and all I see is cloudy emptiness.

God is always near, but sometimes we find that hard to believe. Our inner blindness is not of God's doing but comes rather from our own failure to stay close to God. God doesn't want distance between us. God is constantly near, waiting for us to respond to God's call. All we need to do is open our hearts and invite God in.

Jesus said, "I send the promise of my Father upon you."
    –Luke 24:49 RSV
Come near to God and he will come near to you.
    –James 4:8 NIV
The Lord is near to all who call on him.
    –Ps. 145:18 NRSV
O God, you are my God; I earnestly search for you. My soul thirsts for you.
    –Ps. 63:1 NLT

As a deer longs for flowing streams, so my soul longs for you, O God.
    –Ps. 42:1 NRSV
Let me abide in your tent forever, find refuge under the shelter of your wings.
    –Ps. 61:4 NRSV
How lovely is your dwelling place, O Lord Almighty. I long . . . to enter the courts of the Lord. With my whole being, body and soul, I will shout joyfully to the living God.
    –Ps. 84:1-2 NLT

Prayer

I hunger for your presence, Lord. I thirst for your waters of righteousness and everlasting life. I long to feel again the precious comfort of your everlasting arms upholding me, your hand leading me, your heart encompassing me. Jesus, send your Holy Spirit to surround my everyday life, that I may serve you well, basking steadily in the radiance of your magnificent grace and love.

Forgiveness When I Feel Guilty or Unforgiven

I spread the word about my sister's marital problems, and I'm not sure she will ever forgive me. That auto accident was my fault; if I don't speak up, I am cheating the victim's insurance company. I lied to someone I didn't want to see, and now I must cover up the first falsehood with more lies. I lost my temper with my insolent child and slapped him in the face.

None of us is perfect or blameless. We all must face the consequences of our wrongdoings. But God knows that we are weak and need his help. Whatever our error, large or small, God forgives us. God paid the price for *all* our failures on the cross. If we truly trust that act of total forgiveness God made on our behalf, we must in turn forgive ourselves–even if our victims do not forgive us. And we must also be willing to forgive those who sin against us.

Jesus said, "Father, forgive them; for they do not know what they are doing."
   –Luke 23:34 NRSV
Happy are those whose transgression is forgiven, whose sin is covered. Happy are those to whom the Lord imputes no iniquity.
   –Ps. 32:1-2 NRSV

O Lord, be gracious to me; heal me, for I have sinned against you.
   –Ps. 41:4 NRSV
Hide your face from my sins.
   –Ps. 51:9 NRSV
The Lord said, "I will be merciful toward [my people's] iniquities, and I will remember their sins no more."
   –Heb. 8:12 RSV
"Your sins are forgiven. . . . Your faith has saved you; go in peace."
   –Luke 7:48, 50 NRSV

Prayer

Lord, I caused someone trouble. I let that person down and I let you down. I am truly sorry I have caused them and myself misery, and because I have caused you pain. I am your child, and I did not honor you by my actions. I do not merit your mercy, Lord, but I know your love is there for me, regardless. Forgive me then so I can pick myself up and serve you and your world again in a humble spirit of forgiven love.

Worth When I Feel Worthless

I look in the mirror, and I don't like what I see. I had a fight with my spouse yesterday and wonder how my spouse could still love me after the way I lashed out. I don't have a very good job, and I don't have the brainpower to do any better. My house looks forever disheveled; I am a lousy homemaker.

Dissatisfactions with ourselves and our lots in life plague all of us at times. Society has set a certain standard for "success." But God's idea of success differs totally from humankind's. God considers each human being precious. God's marvelous plan for the unique courses of our lives is determined by the differing gifts God gives us. Most of all, we find priceless worth just in being loved by God, as we are.

When I look at your heavens, the work of your fingers, . . . what are human beings that you are mindful of them . . . ? Yet you have made them a little lower than God, and crowned them with glory and honor.
    –Ps. 8:3-5 NRSV
I praise you, for I am fearfully and wonderfully made.
    –Ps. 139:14 NRSV

Your eyes beheld my unformed substance. In your book were writ-
ten all the days that were formed for me, when none of them as yet
existed.
　　–Ps. 139:16 NRSV
The Lord says, "I have called you by name, you are mine."
　　–Isa. 43:1 RSV
Everyone who is called by my name . . . I created for my glory.
　　–Isa. 43:7 NIV
Once you were no people but now you are God's people.
　　–1 Pet. 2:10 RSV

Prayer

Lord, when I look at what I am and have, I often see what is miss-
ing. "If only I were talented or beautiful or popular," I think to
myself. I sometimes wonder if I'm any good at all. But when I think
that way, I am not seeing with your eyes. Help me to recognize all
my traits as gifts from you, designed for your purposes, part of your
magnificent plan for my life. Make me your beautifully faithful servant, capable of serving you and humanity as you would have me
do so, in big ways or small.

Hope When I Feel Hopeless

At work I've been passed over time after time; I don't think I'll ever get promoted. My bills are so high, I'll never get out of debt. The doctors just can't seem to find the source of my pain. I don't think my spouse and I will ever be able to work out our marital difficulties.

Sometimes problems grow into mountains that appear impassable. Discouragement pyramids into hopelessness. God does not want us to feel hopeless. Jesus came to *bring* us hope. In walking with God through all difficulties, we will find our hope.

Lord, where do I put my hope? My only hope is in you.
    –Ps. 39:7 NLT
Surely I know the plans I have for you, says the Lord, plans for your welfare and not for harm, to give you a future with hope.
    –Jer. 29:11 NRSV
Our Lord Jesus Christ . . . has given us new birth into a living hope through the resurrection.
    –1 Pet. 1:3 NIV

I will wait for the Lord ... and I will hope in him.
  –Is. 8:17 RSV
Be strong and take heart, all you who hope in the Lord.
  –Ps. 31:24 NIV
*The God of hope [will] fill you with all joy and peace in believing,
so that you may abound in hope by the power of the Holy Spirit.*
  –Rom. 15:13 NRSV

Prayer

Lord, I can't see an end to my misery. But that's the trouble: I have
tried to solve my own problems instead of leaving them in your
hands. You know the plans you have for me, and you have offered
to take on my burdens. Help me entrust my daily walk and destiny
to you. For in doing so, I will find the blessing of boundless hope in
you, my wise and glorious Lord and Savior.

A Sense of Purpose When I Feel Aimless

There is no point in giving serious thought to my company's objectives; I probably won't be here long enough to see them through. I can't plan ahead for retirement; I never know from year to year how much social security will be there. What will I do when I retire? I may not even be in this community. In fact, I don't have any goals. How can a person plan on anything these days?

In today's rapidly changing world, it is hard to set personal goals. "What is my purpose for living?" we ask ourselves. Only in God's world will we find the answers. When God's purposes for our lives become the focus of our own missions and goals, we find our answers.

When God desired to show even more clearly to the heirs of the promise the unchangeable character of his purpose, he guaranteed it by an oath, so that . . . [we] might be strongly encouraged to seize the hope set before us.

   –Heb. 6:17-18 NRSV

[Lord,] do not let me stray from your commands. . . . I will meditate on your precepts and consider your ways. I will delight in your decrees.

   –Ps. 119:10, 15-16 NIV

Your hand shall lead me, and your right hand shall hold me fast.
    –Ps. 139:10 NRSV
I know the plans I have for you, says the Lord.
    –Jer. 29:11 RSV
Nothing you do for the Lord is ever useless.
    –1 Cor. 15:58 NLT
What is due me is in the Lord's hand, and my reward is with my God.
    –Isa. 49:4 NIV

Prayer

Lord, I need not wander aimlessly, wondering what my mission in life is. Your will for living everyday life was written down for your people thousands of years ago. If I study your word, follow your will as you make it known to me, and seek your righteousness, my life will not only honor you but also will be a blessing to me and everyone around me. Send your spirit into my life to so lead me.

Satisfaction When I Am Disenchanted

I thought when we married we would be blissfully happy. If this is my dream job, why isn't it satisfying me? This treatment was supposed to solve all my medical problems, but it didn't. I thought skiing would be lots of fun, but I get too tired climbing back up the hills again and again.

Are your aspirations turning into disappointments? Have you become disenchanted with some part of your life? God knows our dreams. God wants to meet the desires of our hearts. But God knows what is best for us, and that is not always what we think is best. In God's dreams and aspirations for us, we will find enduring satisfaction.

God speaks again and again, though people do not recognize it. He speaks in dreams, in visions of the night when deep sleep falls on people as they lie in bed.
    –Job 33:14-15 NLT
God says, "Listen, listen to me, and eat what is good, and your soul will delight in the richest of fare."
    –Is. 55:2 NIV
One thing have I asked of the Lord, that I will seek after; to live in the house of the Lord all the days of my life, to behold [his] beauty.
    –Ps. 27:4 NRSV

How lovely is your dwelling place, O Lord Almighty! Blessed are those who dwell in your house.
    –Ps. 84:1, 4 NIV

Whatever is honorable, whatever is just, whatever is pure, whatever is lovely, whatever is gracious, if there is any excellence, if there is anything worthy of praise, think about these *things.*
    –Phil. 4:8 RSV [emphasis added]

Prayer

Lord, I keep running down alleys, only to find they are dead ends. I often wonder why life is not more promising. It is probably because my dreams center on society's promises, not yours. You know what will truly give me a beautiful life. It cannot be based on earthly ways and values, for they all disappoint sooner or later. Instead, help me find my satisfaction in life by serving you and my fellow human beings in ways that honor you and reflect your view of what "the good life" is all about.

Compassion When I Am Downhearted

My heart is heavy. I can't feel the sun's warmth, even though it's a mild, sunny day. We split up; I love her, but she didn't love me. My promised job didn't come through. The divorce is going through; we just couldn't work things out. My best friend is moving thousands of miles away.

Some life problems are crushing. We wonder if our broken hearts will ever heal. But they do. God is a healer and an ever-present source of compassionate love, day and night, whatever our burden, wherever we are, whenever we need God. That's a promise we can surely count on.

I am like an owl of the wilderness, like a little owl of the waste places. I lie awake; I am like a lonely bird on the housetop. . . . My days are like an evening shadow; I wither away like grass.
    –Ps. 102:6-7, 11 NRSV
Why are you cast down, O my soul, and why are you disquieted within me? Hope in God.
    –Ps. 42:5 NRSV
The Lord is close to the broken-hearted; he rescues those who are crushed in spirit.
    –Ps. 34:18 NLT

[The Lord] has rescued us from the dominion of darkness and brought us into the kingdom of the Son he loves.
  –Col. 1:13 NIV
You, O Lord, are a compassionate and gracious God, slow to anger, abounding in love and faithfulness.
  –Ps. 86:15 NIV
By day the Lord directs his love, at night his song is with me–a prayer to the God of my life.
  –Ps. 42:8 NIV

Prayer

The problems of life are crushing in on me, Lord. My soul is disquieted. I need you to rescue me. I long for the continual reassurance of your love during my daytimes and the compassionate music of your voice during the nights. Heal my heavy heart. Lift my spirit in humble obedience to you. And turn my mournful tunes into joyful songs of praise at the sheer privilege of living with and for you, my everlastingly faithful God.

God's Offer
of Gifts
for My Heart

Companionship When I Feel Lonely

I miss my husband terribly since he died. I didn't want to move so far away from my family. I wish my job didn't require so much travel. I never realized how lonely I would be once the children were gone from home.

Loneliness strikes at our hearts with an ache that just won't go away. God doesn't want human beings to be lonely. He said so when he created the first person, Adam, before sin ever came into the world. But in an imperfect world, loneliness happens. With God's help, we can find new companions to share our joys and sorrows. In the meantime, he can and will fill our empty hearts. He promises to do so. Those who abide in him never walk alone.

The Lord God said, "It is not good that the man should be alone; I will make him a helper as his partner."
    –Gen. 2:18 NRSV
Jesus said, "Abide in me as I abide in you."
    –John 15:4 NRSV
"Anyone who comes to me I will never drive away."
    –John 6:37 NRSV
"Remember, I am with you always, to the end of the age."
    –Matt. 28:20 NRSV

"I will never leave you or forsake you."
  –Heb. 13:5 NRSV

Ruth said to her widowed mother-in-law Naomi: "Where you go, I will go; Where you lodge, I will lodge; your people shall be my people, and your God my God."
  –Ruth 1:16 NRSV

[Lord,] even though I walk through the darkest valley, . . . you are with me.
  –Ps. 23:4 NRSV

Prayer

It is too quiet in my house, Lord. I long for someone with whom I could share intimately my joys and sorrows. There is no human being here, but I know you always are. Fill me with your presence. Give me words to pour out to you the loneliness in my heart. If it be your will, provide new companions to fill the emptiness I feel. But wherever I go and with whom, surround my spirit with the fullness of your spirit's presence, that my soul may sing again marvelous songs of praise and thankfulness to you–my loving, ever present God.

A Sense of Belonging When I Feel Rootless

A tornado blew apart my house. My family gradually disbanded. I lost our family records in a fire. I moved far away from my close relatives, and now I can't get back for holidays and other family gatherings.

Some circumstances of life uproot us from our personal moorings. Roots are important. They give us security, a sense of belonging. But nothing on earth is sure. Our only indestructible roots are those grounded in being part of God's kingdom. We followers belong to God. God is our absolute security–always there for us and with us. God's people are our spiritual family. And God's home, on earth as in heaven, is our everlasting home.

We have [in our hope in Christ] a sure and steadfast anchor of the soul.
   –Heb. 6:19 NRSV
Because of Christ, we have received an inheritance from God . . . . [Christ] has purchased us to be [God's] own people.
   –Eph. 1:11, 14 NLT

"I am the vine, you are the branches."
    –John 15:5 NASB
[Father,] I made your name known to them, and I will make it known, so that the love with which you loved me may be in them, and I in them.
    –John 17:26 NRSV
Since we are all one body in Christ, we belong to each other, and each of us needs all the others.
    –Rom. 12:5 NLT

Prayer

Right now I feel as though I don't belong anywhere, Lord. But that's not true. I am now and always your child and a member of your family because I love you and want to follow you to the end of my days. Send me your Holy Spirit to assure me that I belong to you and to your people. We have a royal destiny, and I have a place in that. I want to celebrate that fact and to reflect it in my everyday life, with and for you and my Christian family.

Understanding When I Feel Misunderstood

Why did my spouse and I lock horns again this morning? Why can't I make my boss understand what I am doing? Why is my best friend mad at me when I was only trying to help? I aim to make myself clear, but sometimes the words don't say what I want to say. How can I ever get my thoughts, feelings, and ideas across accurately?

Communication is an inexact science. Part of the problem is that we humans don't even understand ourselves very well. But God understands, and God promises to help us get through–to God as well as to others. If we ask, God will give us the words to say or lead us onto paths where words are not necessary.

O Lord, you have searched me and known me. . . . You discern my thoughts from far away. . . . Even before a word is on my tongue, O Lord, you know it completely.
    –Ps. 139:1-2, 4 NRSV
Give me understanding that I may live.
    –Ps. 119:144 NIV

The Spirit helps us in our weakness; . . . [and] intercedes for us with sighs too deep for words.
   –Rom. 8:26 RSV
Let the words of my mouth and the meditation of my heart be acceptable to you, O Lord, my rock and my redeemer.
   –Ps. 19:14 NRSV
Now go; I will help you speak and will teach you what to say.
   –Exod. 4:12 NIV

Prayer

Lord, I wish I could make people understand me. I want to be heard, but so often my words don't say what I want to say. Or if they do, sometimes the words are hurtful. Give me the words to communicate lovingly and effectively with those I love, work with, or deal with, so that all of my speech–or my silence–may reflect your grace in my life and thus honor you, my Lord and Savior.

A Forgiving Spirit When I've Been Mistreated or Wronged

I didn't deserve that cutting remark my friend made. My spouse shouldn't have left me out of such an important decision. Despite what my teenager says, I am *not* a thoughtless, cruel parent! I did not punch my neighbor, as he claims; this matter should never have come to court.

Sometimes thoughtlessly, sometimes intentionally, injustices happen. They happened to Jesus, too. Sometimes they don't get corrected here on earth, but God is just. Sooner or later he will right all wrongs. In the meantime, God's understanding love and support will help us deal with our hurts. But God also wants us to forgive our enemies, for our sakes as well as theirs.

Vindicate me, O God, and defend my cause; . . . from those who are deceitful and unjust deliver me!
   –Ps. 43:1 NRSV
Many seek the favor of a ruler, but it is from the Lord that one gets justice.
   –Prov. 29:26 NRSV
[The Lord] will bring forth your vindication as the light, and your right as the noonday.
   –Ps. 37:6 RSV

[Love] does not seek its own, is not provoked, does not take into account a wrong suffered. . . . [It] bears all things.
    –1 Cor. 13:5, 7 NASB

Make sure that nobody pays back wrong for wrong, but always try to be kind.
    –1 Thess. 5:15 NIV

[Joseph, to his murderous brothers:] Do not be afraid, for am I in God's place? . . . you meant evil against me, but God meant it for good.
    –Gen. 50:19-20 NASB

Prayer

When people are deceitful or unkind to me, I get very upset, Lord. Injustice is not your way, so I'm sure it makes you unhappy, too. Help me to forgive the faults of others, as you do mine, helping me to see that some good may be involved. In your hands may I turn the wrongs they do into opportunities to share with them your forgiving mercy, love, and grace.

Freedom When I Feel Oppressed

My company is putting heavy pressure on me to work harder and put in longer hours. My wife makes me feel like a slave in my own home. My parents still try to run my life, and I don't know how to stop them without hurting them. My children wear me down with their constant demands.

People take advantage of others, sometimes intentionally, sometimes unawares. Being on the receiving end can leave us feeling tyrannized. God does not want this for us. If we ask, God will help lighten our load and find the freedom we need to serve God and humanity well. In trying, long-lasting circumstances, God will help us bear up. We honor God in doing so.

Be gracious to me, O God, for people trample on me.
    –Ps. 56:1 NRSV
Do not let me be disgraced, or let my enemies rejoice in my defeat.
    –Ps. 25:2 NLT
The Lord is a stronghold for the oppressed.
    –Ps. 9:9 NRSV

Rescue me from those who pursue me. . . . Set me free from my prison that I may praise your name.
    –Ps. 142:6-7 NIV
The Lord works vindication and justice for all who are oppressed.
    –Ps. 103:6 NRSV
Whatever you do, do everything for the glory of God.
    –1 Cor. 10:31 NRSV

Prayer

It is so hard to see your will in my oppressive circumstances, Lord. I know this is not the way you want things. Fortify me with the will and courage to free myself from those situations where I can. Give me patience and a long-suffering heart for those in which I cannot. Whatever the conditions, I need not worry for, ultimately, you are in control. Your plan for me and those around me is what matters. I thank you with all my heart that, no matter where my journey takes me, you are always there with me.

Reward When I Feel Unappreciated

My family takes me for granted. My children never thank me for any of the sacrifices I am making in raising them. My employer expects me to work overtime and considers it "just part of the job." I went out of my way to help my friend when she was sick, and she never even thanked me.

Gratitude is not in good supply in present-day society, but then it never has been. God understands how lack of appreciation feels. Only one of the ten lepers whom Jesus healed came back to thank God [Luke 17:12]. In this world we may never receive our due, but we can resolve to let others know how much we appreciate them. And we will always find reward in knowing that our Lord loves our every good act. It is God who matters most.

[Someday] the Son of Man is going to come in his Father's glory with his angels, and then he will reward each person according to what he has done.

–Matt. 16:27 NIV

Jesus says, "When you [care for] one of the least of these my brothers and sisters, you [are] doing it to me."

–Matt. 25:40 NLT

We are made right with God by what we do, not by faith alone. . . .
Faith is dead without good deeds.
    –James 2:24, 26 NLT
He who sows righteousness reaps a sure reward.
    –Prov. 11:18 NIV
A capable wife who can find? She is far more precious than jewels. . . .
A woman who fears the Lord is to be praised.
    –Prov. 31:10, 30 NRSV
The Lord loves the righteous.
    –Ps. 146:8 RSV

Prayer

Even when I feel unappreciated, Lord, you are aware of my kind deeds, and you care. Help me to be grateful to you for every blessing you give, whether food or freedom or just your presence in my life. Thank you for my loved ones, for the gift of their presence. And keep me forever thankful, whatever my circumstances, for you are always there–loving me and supporting my walk through life.

Faithfulness When I Feel Betrayed

My friend said she would never tell! My fiancé broke off our engagement. My wife was flirting with that man. How could my children decide to live with my ex-spouse, after all I've done for them? The company promised *me* that job!

People make commitments and then don't keep them. Betrayal hurts. It is one of the most difficult of all life experiences to accept. But Jesus understands; he was betrayed by his best friends. He will heal our hurting hearts and, being forever faithful, will never let us down. More than that, he wants us to forgive our betrayers, as he did. For only then will we be completely healed and restored to true fullness of living.

Jesus says, "You will be betrayed even by parents and brothers, by relatives and friends. . . . By your endurance you will gain your souls."
   –Luke 21:16, 19 NRSV
Many a man proclaims his own loyalty, but a faithful man who can find?
   –Prov. 20:6 RSV
Father, forgive these people, because they don't know what they are doing.
   –Luke 23:34 NLT

God is faithful.
    −1 Cor. 1:9 RSV
Let us hold fast the confession of our hope without wavering, for he who promised [our salvation] is faithful.
    −Heb. 10:23 RSV
When you are praying, first forgive anyone you are holding a grudge against, so that your Father in heaven will forgive your sins, too.
    −Mark 11:25 NLT

Prayer

Lord, sometimes others betray our trust, and we don't know where to turn. Or do we? You are forever faithful. We can trust in you and your promises without reservation. In truth, all of us humans fall short of your glory. Help me to forgive those who have betrayed me even as you have forgiven me. For then my betrayers and I will be able to live together again in your kind of trust—the faith in others that blesses us and everyone around us. All to the praise of your glorious name.

Eternal Comfort When I Am Grief-Laden

I just can't get past the loss of my spouse. My dog died, and I miss my little buddy constantly. I never thought losing the farm would be so hard. The doctor says I'll never get back the use of my arm. I will never again be able to find a job as challenging and satisfying as the one I just left.

Losses come in many forms, major and minor. But they have this in common: losses don't come back. Something we treasured is gone forever. God cares about us and what we have lost. At these times, if we but ask, God will comfort and heal our saddened hearts. We have God's compassionate concern for as long as we need it. It is there for us, forever.

Blessed are those who mourn, for they will be comforted.
    –Matt. 5:4 NRSV
[When his friend Lazarus died,] Jesus wept.
    –John 11:35 RSV
Precious in the sight of the Lord is the death of his faithful ones.
    –Ps. 116:15 NRSV

My soul finds rest in God alone.
   –Ps. 62:1 NIV
My soul is satisfied as with a rich feast . . . when I think of you [Lord] on my bed, and meditate on you in the watches of the night.
   –Ps. 63:5-6 NRSV
You hold me by my right hand. You guide me with your counsel, and afterward you will take me into glory.
   –Ps. 73:23-24 NIV

Prayer

The losses of life are so hard to bear. Comfort me, Lord, with the knowledge that you care, that you cry with me. I know that this is a part of life. Various kinds of losses are with us throughout our lives. But there is one comfort that will always return us to life at its very best–the knowledge that we will someday see eternal union with you and all our faithful loved ones in heaven. Whenever my future seems bleak, be with me and help me to focus on your magnificent eternal destiny for me.

Index

Other Resources from Augsburg

Psalms for Healing by Gretchen Person
176 pages, 0-8066-4161-4

A thoughtful collection of the most helpful passages from the psalms for those seeking healing. Organized by specific emotions, situations, and events, this is a resource that patients, family, and caregivers will treasure and use.

When You Have a Chronic Illness by Margaret Houk
48 pages, 0-8066-4373-0

This book combines expert professional advice with the experiences of the author and other chronically ill persons to show readers effective ways to face and transcend obstacles.

Prayers for Help and Healing by William Barclay
128 pages, 0-8066-2784-0

For people in crisis and their caregivers, William Barclay has written these simple, practical, and comforting prayers. Included are prayers for sickness, pain, anxiety, every aspect of hospital life, holidays, and other times.

Welcoming Change by James E. Miller
64 pages, 0-8066-3338-7

An insightful, compassionate exploration of the experience of change told with simple, affirming suggestions for managing life's transitions. Includes beautiful full-color nature photographs that suggest hope and strength.

Available wherever books are sold.
To order these books directly, contact:
1-800-328-4648 • www.augsburgbooks.com
Augsburg Fortress, Publishers
P.O. Box 1209, Minneapolis, MN 55440-1209